Dancing with the daisies

Saba Shafi

XXX

Woven Words Publishers OPC Pvt. Ltd.

Registered Office:

Vill: Raipur, P.O: Raipur Paschimbar,

Dist: Purba Midnapore, Pin: 721401,

West Bengal, India.

www.wovenwordspublishers.in

Email: editor@wovenwordspublishers.net

First published by Woven Words Publishers OPC Pvt. Ltd., 2017

Copyright© Saba Shafi, 2017

POETRY

ISBN 13: 978-93-86897-09-1

ISBN 10: 9386897091

Price: ₹200/$10

Printed and bound in India

Acknowledgement

As I set out scribbling in my journal, incoherently at first, dribbling slowly, or spurting violently, little could I realise when and how, my poems attained the fluidity and rhythm of a gently flowing river (roaring in foamy mouthfuls at times) trailing the mountainous valley, back home in Kashmir. In the melting of icy glaciers, in the dreary dark winters of lost faith and discovered love, in the extinction of blurred candles of hope and in the dimness of newly dreamt dreams, in the thawing of frozen hearts, this book was born. Embedded richly within the bosom of metaphors, poetry reveals as much as it conceals, it's power glaringly manifest and enigmatically latent. Draped thus, in words and in silence, is my very first attempt at stringing words and images together, all stemming from my heart.

And in this roller coaster of a journey, I thank all those that have been and continue to be, by my side or in my thoughts.

Manan, who adds meaning to all I do, nothing could be possible without you taking care of everything I can possibly think of (and even what I don't). Mama, Baba, Junaid, for all the love and sarcasm that keeps me going. Ma, Daddy and the rest of the family and friends for being supportive always.

Suhail Naqshbandi (Swear By Design), whose art and creativity I can swear by, for putting together this wonderful cover in such little time.

Lastly and most importantly, to my readers who are willing to journey with me, I wish you a fulfilling ride.

Saba Shafi Makhdoomi

Chicago, 7 December, 2017.

For Mama, who bore her seed with patience

A harvest of new crops

She tries to speak to herself through the distance

That long, long chasm separating her from her

A thick barrier of dust and haze, an unscalable wall she
must climb

One that impedes her voice from reaching her own ears

Obstructing, barricading hearts from hearts.

She uses both hands to wipe away the mist

That thick fog of unspoken, unheard words

Settling on this mirror of fragile hearts

Dense cobwebs form too, intricately woven

With the depths of her stricken mind.

A gentle sprinkle of kindness is showered

Repeatedly, painstakingly, patiently too

A soothing balm applied on sore wounds, rubbed gently

To revive and blow life into the decadent soul.

Bodies are exhumed from old, unnamed graves

Graves are re-dug and the dead put back to sleep again

Tiny lumps of misshapen moist mud picked up from the banks

To carve hopes of hopes and dreams of dreams

New words must, however, be learnt

New stories have to be woven

New yarns spun by old decrepit hands…

Tales of beauty and grace and joy

Of silken threads, silver and gold

Flowy gowns embracing her body

Wrapping her greys in the dim pallid moonlight

The greys of her tresses and her heart, both

The fabric of her soul is unwound and disentangled

Threadbare now, to be rewoven thread by thread

Faded tones, now bleached forever

Squeezed and wrung, hung up to dry in the fading sun

And all colour is drained from her blanched lips too.

Now, colourless, untouched, reborn, pure

To be immersed in tones, more humble and subdued.

Dull gold of the sad afternoon skies, perhaps?

Or soft peach of her playful cheeks?

Or olives and pistachios that touched her mouth

Tongue rolled around those words, coloured then

Colourless now

Bitten lips, chewed up feelings and lines spat out

Sucked dry of all meanings, shallow or profound

Yet a flickering hope, you see?

Of the Source still living on

Under the shade of the bare wiry tree?

This winter might be long and cold and dry,

Yet the snow will melt and the rivers will swell

And hot springs will gush forth, piercing the soil of her
soul

A harvest of new words might crop up then

From those lips and from her veins....

The magic of alchemy

She chases wild dreams on dull, winter afternoons

The smoke and haze not dimming her sight

Tiny fireflies light up her vision

Magical lanterns straddle her path.

She grasps and hugs the light spring air

Wraps it around her shoulders for warmth

And spreads her arms to embrace chimeras

Fierce dragons that breathe forked tongues of fire.

What then becomes of dreams dreamt in the depths of dark nights?

Dreams that gleamed and glowed and shone in her eyes?

Piercing the darkness by its own radiance

Darting right past her droopy eyes

Eyes that twitched in its blazing incandescence

Lay flickering now, as dreams were snuffed out in one
strong puff

Circling rings of smoke float past her sleepy head

She coaxes and cajoles and wheedles the unruly beast

Climbs up its steep, thick scaly back

It abrades her soft hands, scrapes her dimpled knees and
bruises her furrowed forehead

It nibbles, gnaws and bites at her dangling rainbow, that
talisman around her neck

Defiant, unruly and wayward this giant!

It corrodes, erodes and defaces all gold

That lay in the chambers of her deep, dark eyes

And yet?

And yet…

One twitch, a flicker,

It reignites and leaps back to life

That undying dream of the dream of her eye

She ties a satin ribbon round the monster's neck

And befriends the demon, that beguiling fiend!

She hops on its back and unfastens her grip

Palms turned upwards, facing the skies

Her diminutive arms spreading over those enormous
wings

Seated thus, she takes off, ascends and glides

Breaking into spurts of giggles, she laughs, childlike

As each teardrop shed, falls back into her tiny hands

Transformed

Metamorphosed

Becoming warm droplets of honey and gold

And such could be the magic of alchemy, she was told!

Setting the bird free

To keep walking this precarious tightrope that separates

Here from There.

To not letting your mind wander and stray

Onto cold, deserted roads that lead nowhere.

To collect this heap of sadness in one sweeping go

And pour it into an old tin jar, forever locked away.

To cork up this bottle of miseries and woes

And throw it into the sea far, far away

To sieve out the heavy pebbles, one by one by one

And fill one's hands with buoyant joyous grains

To remove that rigid armour encasing her heart

And setting the fluttering bird free…

A rainbow of Hope

As Darkness snuffs out all glimmering candles of Hope

She toils hard to search with that sparkle of her heart

She digs deep using both her hands

To salvage faded shadows of that pale, stolen twinkle

Now obscured by a thick layer of dust

That clouded and blinded her eyes

She peeps through that curtain, slowly but surely

To catch a glimpse, any remnant of beauty.

If only warm droplets that form on her lashes

Could be that gentle drizzle in which all darkness
washes?

And what if?

What if tiny crystalline prisms, limpid and pristine

Could be a window through which rays of light would
stream

Entering thus, through tightly shut eyes?

Each sombre streak bursts into happy hues

A painting of new-born dreams

A rainbow, perhaps?

A rainbow of new hopes pushing through her penumbra

An arc encircling her soft pale shoulders

From 'that left' to this 'right?'

A thousand tinted dreams dreamt, in the blink of an eye!

A thousand lives lived

A thousand songs sung

A thousand seasons seen.

How many paths trodden?

All drenched and sodden!

White little daisies crushed under uncertain strides

New flowers budding where the earth had dried

New dances danced, where music had ceased

New smiles smiled, when the pain had eased

This rainbow formed after a stormy downpour

And she soaks and basks in all those colours

Painting her wide white canvas

In slow strokes of a brush

She, too, paints a rainbow-- small and modest

Beneath which uneasy hearts could rest?

A rainbow of Hope?

Put that to test!

Her feather of gold

She sat by herself journeying back in time

To gather long lost memories of forgotten childhoods

Tiny dimpled fingers curling 'round long slender ones

Frail green tendrils creeping over tall havens

She steps on that ladder that promised all heavens

And retraces imprints in the soft sand of her soul

To rebuild castles of hope with her tiny hands

Yet not lose heart as the waves knock them down

To fly kites of hopes and desires, soaring wildly in the
summer skies

Thread wound firmly over the spool of a dreamer's heart

To let ones gaze wander again

Bursting forth that mist and haze

To a time

When sparkling streams would spurt forth and spout

Unbridled, those words would simply spring out!

Ah! The effusive rush!

A thoughtless outpouring!

That thunderous downpour!

To then dive back in that wetly woven sea?

Reckless! Rash! Hasty! Hurried!

No sails to take her forward, no anchors buried!

To feel ones heart race at deafening speed

As she lunges blindly toward that precipice

With nothing to hold onto, save one delicate feather

Clasped firmly in tiny clutched fists

This light, delicate plume of the hope of a hope.

To plunge into that cold, freezing water

With a heavy rock tied around her neck

She now knew of no hands willing to pull her out

Save her own lone feather keeping her afloat, up and about!

Curtains must fall

Curtains must fall on all such windows that obstructed
her view

And hindered her heart.

Windows, that she naively believed opened inwards

Through which light would reach her, pristine and
filtered.

Windows, she believed could take her places

Laughing, playing, rolling on the lush green meadows…

But that chiasma only carried her warm breath outwards,
sucking her marrow dry

To mix with the dusty haze of exhumed ghosts…

It took with itself all that was glowing and radiant.

Those tiny little stars were plucked from starry skies

Shooting stars caught darting away

Held in hand, they were carelessly caught

And into the void, were cruelly flung away.

Her twinkle was stolen, her flash was plundered

Smiles were looted

Dreams were pilfered…

Of what use could they be?

Removed from eyes that could truly see?

Curtains must be drawn on all mistaken songs

On songs of grief and sorrow.

Curtains must fall, for though this dark, dreary night
seems very long

One can still dream of a new dawn tomorrow….

Dancing with the daisies

She could dance with the daisies, yellow and white

Wild pointed heads sprouting from the earth

She would run barefoot on the dew-kissed grass

Her feet rubbing gently against those soft blades of

Pliable, green swords that could bend and sway with
each stride

Matching her step for step,

Twisting and whirling with her pedal curves and bends

They arched, swayed and swirled with such grace and
ease

As they would in a gently blowing, soft breeze.

She bends over softly, plucking dandelions hidden from
her seeking eyes

Scattered amongst the bushes, untamed and wild

Holding close to her lips, she blows each feathery floret
into the air

The wind carrying those delicate, silvery flakes
everywhere!

With each deep breath, humble prayers were exhaled

Dispersing seeds of hopes into the skies

A handful of sprinkling was showered from those small
hands

In search of a tiny patch, watered and fertile

Where those seeds of hope and prayers would find their
promised lands

And then, embed and bury deep inside the womb of the
earth

Lie dormant, waiting for the cold winters to pass

And with the heralding of spring, germinate, sprout and
grow tall!

It was only beneath her feet that those scattered seeds
would eventually fall

What blossomed and bloomed were daisies and
dandelions

And the answers to all her prayers came in that one call....

She would soon dance with the daisies one more time...

For there has to be a rise after such a sharp fall...

Chasing the comet's tail

To be alive or be fossilized?

To live one life passionately or be mummified a
thousand times?

To exhale hot breath laced with madness or heavy,
leaden air frozen in numbness?

To soar, to fly or sink and die?

To chase, to seek or hide and leave?

To put away things best left unsaid or bend over and
pick up lost threads?

To journey timidly on familiar, known paths or embark
upon rocky, untrodden roads?

To let this light devour all darkness around?

To think a million new thoughts not thought of before?

Or replay old stories, tepidly retold?

To let poisonous arrows pierce her Achilles heel?

Or bend forward and curl up, allowing old wounds to
seal?

To have eager children chase the comet's tail?

Or let shooting stars fade in oblivious tales?

To cover and drape all dreams with a thousand and one
veils?

Or plunge straight into turbulent waters with no mast and
only tattered sails?

To burn one's oar and still hope no more?

Or build new bridges, one creaky plank after another

A bridge that unites two opposite shores…

Weathering a storm

How does one weather a storm?

By walking straight into its arms?

By letting go off all that holds you down?

Or by lying still and drown?

How does one weather a storm?

By freezing and simply looking on?

Or taking this storm by a storm?

Embracing, accepting and fighting

One battle after another

That lone soldier struggling on the front

Was none other but her heart bearing the brunt

Words of wisdom oft repeated…

Like everything else, this too shall end

Patience, O heart, patience my friend!

All answers shall reach the heart

To run a race against Time?

Backward, forward in one frantic leap?

Heaping piles and piles of wasted years

Then packing them all up in one big bundle

To dump it underneath that sea…

The waves tide over

Taking it farther away

The sand…That silt…That shadow…The guilt

The moon, my heart

His soul, my eclipse

My moon overshadowed by his overbearing soul

The heart eclipsed by that staggering shadow…until it
slowly recedes away

To now search for a new space within this Space?

A tiny niche to place her lamp?

A corner of her own?

A place that would bring a flicker of respite

Her silent refuge, the cradle of a mother's lap

Her tired head placed gently, lovingly

With tender fingers running softly through her hair

Smoothening the tangles formed inside her knotty head

One comforting hug and all-time freezes

Her head bogged down by all that weight

Soaks in whatever strength it can

From every pore, each little touch

Every careful glance cast upon her…

Solace sought in heads kissing the floor

Where both bodies and souls jointly prostrate

Humble heads kneeling down slowly

And earnest arms being raised plaintively...

The voice that rises from such deep caverns

Has a way of finding its way up, through the tempest?

All answers shall reach the heart in the end

For a Hand picks you up once you bend

The heart will find its way

When the clouds would have drifted away

And each burden wearing the heart down, vanish away

When all tattered memories would bury underneath
winter's first snow

That is when the heart would magically know

It will find its way...

Find its way home...

When the oft trodden paths would have left no trails
behind

No track to trace the journey even in the mind

For sudden, blissful rains would have washed it all away

The clear skies would then bear testimony

And in resonance, those tall poplars would sway

That is when she would know

The heart will find its way…

Find its way home…

When those silences would have transformed into music

And curled up, withered bodies would open up to lost grace

When those shadows would have disappeared forever

And darkness would give way to a light so bright

That is when she would know

Know it well and know it right

The heart will find its way

When her entangled hair would have straightened out

But those soft, gentle waves would still remain

Both in her tresses and in her heart

Flowing freely in the morning breeze,

in harmony both within and without

That's when she would know for sure

The heart will find its way out

When the fire of anguish would have burnt itself out

And searing, burning desires washed away

Neither one shall last, nor the other remain

That's when the heart would silently know

It's time to move on, time to go

To leap out of the chest that caged it so

The heart would have found its way then...

Found its way back home...

The haunted house

That lone, dilapidated monstrosity still stood

Even as those wooden beams rotted away

Gnawed at, devoured by termites barrelling their way in

Slowly, imperceptibly biting away

Biting their way into her soft flesh

Biting their way into a susceptible heart

Yet she remained a captive in that house

Inches away from being razed to the ground

Incarcerated in a prison that caged her heart

That haunted house…deserted…desolate

Windows smeared with the black of dark nights

Clamped tight

Doors locked, leaving her no escape…

She pulls all drawers out, one after the other

And abandoned memories leap out at her

Its sting penetrates her black eyes

She cringes and shuts each drawer back

Fear stricken she freezes, deathly white

She is a ghost wading past a graveyard of memories

A hapless captive of her own heart…

Shall we dream new dreams?

Shall we dream new dreams,

Even though our eyes are bleary and fatigued?

Dream dreams of new sunrises,

Even as we witness the sun setting down?

Dream of new beginnings,

Even as the end seems within reach?

Dream of lives lived in a blink,

A blink that lasts an eternity...

Dream of caged eagles set free

After years of miserable bondage...

Of new wings sprouting and spreading,

Even as the old ones lay broken on the ground...

Dream of grey skies turning blue,

That canopy of love spread out for you...

Dream of that secret place deep inside,

Where calm and tranquillity shall finally reside...

Dream of those idyllic mustard fields sprawling on either
side,

Embraced softly by the sharpness of those mountains,

And that long, straight road slicing those fields in two,

That artery branching straight from the heart,

With blood coursing from me to you...

That lone metallic bridge with frothy, foaming river
rushing underneath

The bridge that had once bridged the dark abyss, those
cracks developed between broken hearts...

The aging, yet formidable chinar stood lone and tall,

Splitting that oft taken path into two,

Its roots boring, burying deep underneath

How many stories had its rustling leaves

whispered in the ears of the passers-by?

How many had it thrown on divergent paths?

And how many, in its shade, were destined to unite?

All in the Eye

All visions were envisaged in the Eye

The fire of Hell and Paradise divine

Grotesque, gory faces, unmasked, unveiled

And dainty, exquisite beauty, hidden, concealed

All secrets were buried deep within one's Eye…

The gossamer veil floating about her

Or the coarse, black shroud blanketing her

The key to all closed doors lay in that tiny opening

The power to transform was in the Eye…

All magic and desire stemmed from that place

Abhorrence and revulsion were seen from it too

Both occult and unveiled danced in those blazing flames

The Hidden and Manifest both resided there

One moment king

One moment beggar

These answers could be sought nowhere else

For they sprang forth from the depths of those dark
Wells…

Not you. Nor him. Neither could I

Ever imagine the reason why

All visions could be envisaged only in the Eye….

The garden of hope

Beauty could be found in unusual places

In a stranger's smile

In kind words sprinkled upon hearts unknowingly

Unexpected cool breeze flowing from unseen corners

Parched lands suddenly soaked with a shower of rain

And gardens blooming in no time

Those bright meadows of lilies and orchids

Of lacy hopes and friable dreams

Where clouds were laid beneath her feet

Where birds sang songs of joy and laughter

Into the convolutions of her ear…

Where sunrises were glorious,

And sunsets divine

Where hearts were unfettered

And hopes soared high

Where wings could be spread far and wide

Spanning the vast expanse of dark skies

Now lit up by lanterns of hope

Shining, bright and radiant in those eyes

As kind smiles would slowly replace cold sighs

Onwards, in that garden she drifted along

Are you mad?

Are you mad?

Well, I am 'real' if that counts?

Are you mad again!

I'm raw, never really could feign…

And that's the whole tragedy!

Laughed the sane

All this 'honesty', this humbug!

What purpose does it serve?

Who stands to gain?

Surely, you must be…

Wildly insane!

Castles on the soil of the soul...

When that 'other 'inside me crumbles to dust

I see those mounds of ruins settling on my feet

No strength could I summon in my entire being

To kick that withered dust away…

It stays…that sad pathetic pile around my feet

Those dunes that had once carried my imprint

Even the westward wind could not

Blow those shadows of dust away…

But once I fall onto my knees

With trembling hands, shall that dust be gathered

And Castles would be built once again

On the ground, this time

On the pliant soil of my soul… And not in air

Death of a salesman

To grieve? To mourn?

Be sad and forlorn?

To grieve a death that never took place?

Or mourn the same death over and again?

To cry bitter tears of anguish?

Those rivers that brimmed to the hilt

And overflowed

The deluge that destroyed the cities again?

Who sheds those tears?

Who cried in vain?

Who, then, put that quivering heart to sleep?

Who steadied those trembling hands?

Were I to speak of the throat, that in mutiny arose?

With a hard-dry lump

And all her eloquence froze!

Which ear heard those words

That refused to leave their abode?

Which heart toted it all?

As brick by brick, she unburdened that heavy load?

Once off her chest,

Where would those stories finally rest?

Beneath the warmth of the soil?

That grave was dug in the cold night

With her own shivering hands, she had to toil

To bury the dead in a casket of ivory and gold

That bore no name, no symbol, no sign

For it carried the body of the mute, the silent....

Only voice and words…

No form, no flesh…

The death of the shadow of a person…

A trader of stories

A marauder of tales

Tiny drops of blood dripping, still warm

Drops of illusion distilling from reality

Immiscible liquids finally separating out

Death of a salesman! she finally sighed…

The Search For An Inner Compass

The compass is you

The destination too

The journey inside

The resting place too

The scorching, scalding sun is you

The breezy shade too

The tears soften the heart's soil

The tears are yours

Never to be soiled

The westward wind carries the seeds

The soil is you

The seed too

The wind is yours

Still doubt ye the sprouting of

Love, life, light all in just one?

The cloud would be yours

But so, would be the sun

Some winters would be long, dark, cold

Bringing in its wake no sun

But the faith must remain

For that is what was sown

It sleeps under the belly of the mother

Dormant, hidden, latent

Curled up on itself

Entangled net of eyes, limbs, toes and woes

The wind still blows

Sooner or later

Thawing all that was frozen

Gently unfurling those tiny, soft fingers

Prodding slowly until the earth shakes–

A full-blown stretch, a yawn

Rubbing of eyes

A flower thrown open

A late bloomer on days

Precocious on others

A rose, a daffodil, a daisy

All but one… One… One

No sunny days are precious

If one embraces not the rains

Soaked hearts, drenched dreams

An empty gaze too, I feign

Layers upon layers upon layers

On this heart of mine

Baroque, convoluted, knotty, labyrinthine

The tiny corridor that leads from mine to yours

Dimly lit by a lone candle, blazing feverishly

But one big blow, quiver, jiggle, joggle

One deathly jolt, jounce, judder and shudder

Is that all that takes to snuff this candle out?

The stairs leading upwards to the Heavens

Come crashing down

I cry, I shout, I wail, bemoan

In darkness I grapple, I clasp, I clench

I stumble, I fall

Quaver, tremble, waver, wobble

Down on my knees yet so tall?

In darkness I search for the way back home

What leads me forth is the light of the soul

The soul trapped in the wind, in those mountains

Swaying with the cypress

Being tilled with the saffron fields

The soul left somewhere back home

It's radiance reaching me here, far removed–

Beaming, bedazzling, fiery, luminous.

The Surrender

I stand at Your doorstep

Pray! Don't shoo me away

My heart is heavy and my back bent

Under the terrible weight I carry within

Will You not admit me inside?

For who else can I turn to?

Who else but You?

You are my voice

The silence too

You are the question

The only answer too

You are the oath, the journey and the destination

You are the Beginning of all beginnings

And the End, final and absolute

The earth, it's centre, the axis is You

The light of the sun and the twinkling stars too

You are my only thirst

And a vast spring too

You are the source

The tiny dot

And the whole universe too

You are my prayer

The answer to it too

You are order

Chaos too

Fluid like water

Solid as the mountains

You are Life

You are Death

You are the dusk

And dawn too

You reside in the creases of dirty palms

And in the purity of an angel's heart

You are Timeless

Ageless

Formless

The roots, the trunk, the bark and the sap from You

The branches, the buds, the flowers and the leaves too

You are the skies above

And the land beneath

The waves of the ocean

The shore too

The tiny grains of sand

The oyster, the pearl, the dirt in its eye too

You are the only Life that exists beyond this realm

You are reason

And my doubts too

A hole in my being

The only means to fill it too

The overt and the covert

You are One! Only One!

Yet sprinkled and scattered in everything

You are my ignorance

And all wisdom too

You are my shell

And the kernel too

The lushness of the rain kissed gardens

And the aridity of sunburnt deserts too

The sunrise is you

The sunset too

The laughter on my lips is Yours

The grief in my heart too

You are lightning, the rumbling thunder, the torrential
downpour too

The head, my thoughts, all memory too

The rough contours of my flawed being are Yours

So, shall the smoothness come from You

My eyes are Yours

The vision too

The mind is Yours

The imagination too

You are the Creator

The created too

The destroyer would be You

And the ruins Yours

You are the calm breeze that blows

And devastating tornadoes too

You are the soil, the seed, the sapling too

The clouds, the dew and the rains too

The boat, my boatman and the oar

The ocean, this river and the sea too

All distances spring from You

So, shall the bridges built be yours

All sins are mine

But am I not Yours?

Embrace me! Embrace me!

Take me in Your arms!

For You are my only!

You are my all!

No 'I' shall remain...

The soul shall find peace within

All barriers would be broken

And the spirit shall be set free

When no 'I' shall remain...

The skies shall then meet the earth

All bits and pieces shall then reunite

Spring and autumn and winter and summer bright

Would all be seen side by side

Snowflakes shall fall on the rainbow's arc

No time shall limit the cycle of night and day

When no 'I' shall remain...

Mountains would be moved by those desperate pleas

No storm shall ever plague the sea

No tempest shall be stoked in her tender chest

No memories would be evoked in a diseased head

Her forehead would be smeared no more with that stain

For no 'I' shall remain

Backs would be bent in earnest prayers

Tired foreheads would kiss the ground

Each little kiss planted on the forehead of Destiny

Neither sanity nor insanity shall then remain

No tragedy, no happiness, no joy, no pain

The weaver's balance shall finally attain

That harmony without as within

No hope of reward, no retribution for sin

For no 'I' shall have remained....

That dust on the ground shall be

The dust that I shall see

Within me

The heart shall excavate out all hopes and desires

Expunge, extract, expel, extricate

No meeting with you,

No separation within

For there shall be no you

And no 'I' shall remain

The 'Other'

Who said Love and Hope were to be found elsewhere?

In some 'other', distinct from us

The 'other', that shall miraculously redeem us?

Deliver us back to our truer selves?

Who said we were fragments, bits and halves unto
ourselves

To be made whole only when united with this 'other'?

The 'other', that would snugly wind itself around the
rocky terrain of our hearts?

And cushion our falls and soften our rise?

Who fed these thoughts into the foolish head?

Who said hearts would remain perpetually locked

Until someone else found the key to it?

How simple, how easy would life then be!

To simply wait, caged up and locked,

Hands tied up behind our backs

To be set free by that mysterious 'other'?

But who would liberate this 'other' from its own
confinement?

What if its bondage is as turbulent as is yours?

Where will we then meet, unfettered, unrestrained?

How will we meet?

And just how long shall this wait be?

Is there hope? Still that faint glimmer of hope?

That, one day, shall appear, out of the thin air

A spectre, an apparition, a visitant perhaps?

And all shall then magically fall in place?

Somehow… Just somehow… I know not how

And all meanings shall then be clear

The nameless shall proclaim their names

The ineffable could then be defined

And we could roll our tongues around the intangibles

And taste it like never before?

The formless shall be poured in our cups

And lo and behold! It would crystallize

The inenarrable shall narrate its own story

But who would hold that mighty pen?

Would someone else do it for us?

Can someone else do it for us?

Somehow… Just somehow…I know not how

Is there an 'other' that even exits?

I search and search and search

In that distant, far away horizon

Only to find

No 'other' exists, except inside…

Diminutive on days, on others, expansive and wide

Disparate at times, but blending too

Remember, this

There will be no 'other', other than you!

Conform

I sought love

I found it not

I rebelled

I fought

I lost

I gave up

I cried

I burnt

I died

I bowed

I rose

In Love.

He says, 'Dear beloved, let me inform

In Love, don't rebel, simply conform!'

When silence speaks

Why do you fear silence?

Lest it speaks more clearly

To you than words ever could?

Let it frighten you no more

Give it your sweaty palms

Let it enclose them

Let this silence grow in you

Course through your veins

Slowly, gently

Don't break this flow

Let it know

That your heart can wear

The plain robe of silence too

Cover the nakedness of vulgar words

Drape it in those graceful folds

Braid your long black hair

And weave tales of silence around

Those curves, those bends

Open the knotted ends of words

Untwist, unwind this constricting rope

Free yourself of this noose

Let those fraught, frayed ends loose

What good are words if they don't ease

The mind and heart of all disease?

Come now, bring your lips forth

Drink, drink from this cup!

Having tasted words, now let silence fill you up

Stop all noise inside, stop that thunder, the clamour, the
din

Let the lyrical speech of silence begin....

Be afraid no more, admit this old friend in!

Love

Love is embracing the flawed you

No drug, no high

No escape, no lie

Love is a revolution, no doubt

For it forces one to look deep inside

To draw inwards inside one's shell

Plunge, delve, seek, wander

And then slowly emerge, changed, transformed

Love is forgetting

Forgetting all fables breathed inside

Admitting shade with the sun by its side

Love is the anvil, the hammer, the heated, molten metal
too

Love is the tautness of those muscles that deliver each
blow

Love is the sweat, that dark grease wiped away too

Love is the molten wax, that liquid pain dripping from
you

And the iron mould that sets it too

Love is freedom and bondage separated by a wink

The rising sun is love

And the setting one too

A tiny grain, no more

An expansive ocean, no less

Love promises no permanent abode

No end in sight, no destination reached

The rocky terrain traversed is love, that path, the journey
and your feet

Love is a baring of soul

It is embracing the ugly distortions within

And planting beautiful kisses on it

Love is a rebellion against all instincts

It boils, it roars, it rages, it seethes

But it also calms, it eases, it soothes

Love is a mirror that reflects your all

The sweetness, the rancour, your flights, your fall

Love rubs, it erases, it rusts and corrodes

It then retouches, recoats all that it erodes

Love fixes your feet firmly on the ground

It anchors, it fastens, it clamps and secures

It then wrests all out, uproots and displaces

What is Love? What all is love?

A panacea? A magic potion?

An affliction or an addiction?

A straight, short path connecting two hearts?

Or a serpentine, winding circuit that sets them apart?

Is it a buttress, a pillar, a pivot?

A constant point?

Or the range, the width, the entire gamut?

And where can it be found?

In the heart of some beautiful beloved

Or in the image reflected in your own eyes?

Love is imperfection left untouched

Love is embracing the flawed you

Love is embracing the flawed you....

Love is consistently watering a withering plant....

Love wants consistent watering of even a withering plant....

Water, water!

Until it blooms...

The red fairy duster

Love was in doing, not merely in saying

Love was in holding, not merely in throwing

It was in colouring a hopelessly dull, dreary painting

In anticipating the enormous blankness of the page

Yet dissolving oneself in the sweeping strokes of the
brush

It was both colour and the colourless water in which it
blended

A blind leap of faith taken as one immersed one's all

In the contrasting shades of the embrace of the other

And the wild beating of synchronous hearts

It steadied the shakiness of an unsteady hand

And raked up solid foundations with ease

Love was the rusty iron shackle fettered onto my feet

Carrying the faint memory in its ring

Of the tinkle of my childhood silver anklets

I slowly left both behind

Those rusty shackles, the silver anklets

Tales of childhood and stories of youth

Each morning I entered the same old room

Each day I saw the same shifting rays of the sun

Some days it rained and the earth still smelled the same

Each night the aroma wafted in my kitchen

Each night, her red toe ring glinted against the pallor of
the flour

That dust accidentally sprinkled upon her feet

The mouldy smell of the day welcomed me yet again

And the bland red fairy duster was plucked by weary
nights

Each night, I mused over the dullness of love

Each sombre funeral followed by a mirthful birth

Each night, those tears returned as well

The salty, vast ocean entering my downturned lips

That paleness of the mouth awash with those drops

My cavern of silence and eloquence, both

I pondered, looked around, then peeped inside my heart

Religiously observing this fast of silence

I now, break that fast yet again

And eat the grey dust of my words once more

I digest, chew the cud, belch out and puke

Here was one truth or a lie that would repeatedly dupe

The only truth and the only lie was love… In my breath,
in my sigh

In his hands and in my eyes

Love was the unfounded, irrational belief

In the wisdom of the other yoked with the ignorance of
my own

Love lay not in constructing a mausoleum in the memory
of a beloved

But in building a nest, straw by straw, twig by twig, in a
shared imperfect life

Love was in the firmness of the roots snarled underneath
each other's damp earth

And in the soaring ascents of the spread wings

In the plummeting nosedives, in the sinking descents too

Love was in both…

Roots and wings

Wings and roots

In ownership and in dispossession

In shared laughter and stifled cries

On days it was hatred unmasked

On others, it was beauty unveiled

It was both

Silence and music

Music and silence

The music of silence....

Lost And Found (Haiku)

I searched the deep seas

I dived, sank and lost my all

To find it again

www.ingramcontent.com/pod-product-compliance
Lightning Source LLC
Chambersburg PA
CBHW021138020426
42331CB00005B/824